Whose Tracks Are These?

To my husband, Chris, for patience and support, and to mentors Sing Hanson and Ernest Lussier, with admiration and gratitude.

—H.S.

"In the end,
  we will preserve only what we love,
  we will love only what we understand,
  and we will understand only what we are taught."

Baba Dioum
conservationist from Senegal

International Standard Book Number 1-879373-89-0
Library of Congress Card Catalog Number 94-65087

Published in the United States of America by

Roberts Rinehart Publishers
Post Office Box 666
Niwot, Colorado 80544

Distributed in the U.S. and Canada by Publishers Group West

Book Design by Hyla M. Skudder

Printed in Hong Kong by Colorcorp/Sing Cheong

Typeset in Columbus, OH by Graphic Impressions

Whose Tracks Are These?

A Clue Book of Familiar Forest Animals

By Jim Nail

Illustrations by Hyla Skudder

ROBERTS RINEHART PUBLISHERS

My tracks show I have long toes. What do you think I use them for?
They help me climb trees and run through the branches without falling.

Here are some nutshells. I sat here, holding a nut in my front paws.
I cut the shell open with my sharp teeth so I could eat the nut.
Even if you don't see my tracks, nutshells may tell you I have been here.

The trees in the forest have lots of nuts for me to eat. When I have eaten enough,
I may bury some nuts to save until later. Often I forget the nuts and they grow
into new trees for the forest.

My long, bushy tail is as long as my body and I often carry it curled up.
My fur may be gray, black, or even red.

Who am I?

I am a squirrel.

Look at all my tracks. They are small, but there are many of them.
I'm very busy. Even though it is summer I am gathering lots of nuts, seeds,
and grains so I have enough food to eat all winter.

I am only about four inches long, but I can hold four acorns in special pouches
in my cheeks. After I fill my cheeks, I take this food back to my underground
home called a burrow. My burrow has special rooms to store the food.

See the entrance to my burrow under this tree root?
It is just big enough for me to fit through.

I have five black stripes and four white ones on my back,
but the rest of my fur is reddish brown.

Who am I?

I am a chipmunk.

See how different my tracks are from the tracks of other animals in the forest? I have hooves, not paws, and my tracks are almost heart-shaped.

Did you notice the two sets of tracks here? One set is smaller and spaced closer together, but looks like mine. Why is that? Did you guess that the smaller tracks belong to my baby?

The points of our hooves show which direction we walked. Where did we go and what did we do? We stopped at the stream for a drink of water.

Even though there are many of my kind in the forest, you'll still have to look very carefully to see me. My brown coat and my ability to stand very still make me hard to see in the forest.

When I'm grown up, my shoulder may be taller than you are. Although I'm large, I am very fast and I am very graceful.

Who am I?

I am a deer.

When you see handprints and footprints that look similar to yours only smaller, they are probably mine.

Look for my tracks in mud near a stream or pond. I love the water and often dip my food in it before I eat. Am I washing my food? Am I getting it wet to make it easier to eat? Only I know, and I won't tell!

I eat lots of different foods such as frogs, fish, fruit, nuts, and plants. I even eat some things you would throw away, so you may find my tracks near your garbage cans. No matter how tightly you close them, I can figure out how to open the cans. My nimble fingers can even untie knots.

Don't mistake me for a bandit even though my face looks like I am wearing a mask. Don't mistake me for a small bear, though some people think I look like one. My tracks are very different, and I have a tail with 5 to 10 black rings.

Who am I?

I am a raccoon.

Look closely at these tracks. Do they look like they were made by a dog?
If you get just a quick look at me you might mistake *me* for a dog, too.

I hunt small animals such as mice for my food. Can you tell from these tracks what
happened here? I caught a mouse to take back to my babies, called kits.

When I walk, I place my paws one in front of the other so my tracks form a straight line.

When you're in the forest, especially at the edge of the forest, look carefully.
You might catch a glimpse of my reddish-brown fur — or just my white-tipped bushy
tail as I run into the woods to hide.

Stories and fables about me say I am clever.

Who am I?

I am a fox.

My tracks are two different sizes. My back paws are much larger than my front paws so that I can hop very fast when I need to.

I need to run fast because many animals hunt my kind. I will zig-zag to make it hard to catch me, then dash into the bushes to escape. My large ears help me hear other animals coming so I have more time to get away.

Some of my cousins are raised and kept as pets. But if you see me in the forest, don't try to catch me and take me home. I am a wild animal and belong in the woods.

But I might come to your backyard, especially if you have a garden. I like to eat young plants, especially vegetables.

My white, puffy tail is another clue to who I am.

Who am I?

I am a rabbit.

I am not an animal but I am full of life.

I reach high up in the sky,
down to the ground —
and even below the ground.
But I am not a tree.

In different seasons, I wear different colors.
But I am not a person.

Those who live here sleep, eat, and raise
their young around me.

But I am not a house.

I provide homes to many, many creatures
all across my land.
But I am not a village, town or city.

I bustle with the activity of all these creatures.
But you will have to be very quiet, and
look very carefully.

Spend some time with me and look
for the tracks of all the animals
who live here.

Who am I?

I am the forest.

DATE DUE

MAY 26	JAN 23		
JAN 30	JAN 4		
DeG.	MAR 11		
JAN 19			
FEB 24			
NOV 14			
JAN 12			
JAN 6			